How to Screw the Post Office

by Mr. Unzip

Loompanics Unlimited
Port Townsend, Washington

This book is sold for informational purposes only. Neither the author nor the publisher will be held accountable for the use or misuse of the information contained in this book.

How to Screw the Post Office
© 2000 by Mr. Unzip

All rights reserved. No part of this book may be reproduced or stored in any form whatsoever without the prior written consent of the publisher. Reviews may quote brief passages without the written consent of the publisher as long as proper credit is given.

Published by:
Loompanics Unlimited
PO Box 1197
Port Townsend, WA 98368

Loompanics Unlimited is a division of Loompanics Enterprises, Inc.
1-360-385-2230
E-mail: service@loompanics.com
Web site: www.loompanics.com

Cover art by Bob Crabb

ISBN 1-55950-200-2
Library of Congress Card Catalog 99-068334

Contents

Introduction 1

Chapter One
   "Technology is Our Friend" 5

Chapter Two
   Cut Your Postage Rates in Half 11

Chapter Three
   2¢ Makes Sense 17

Chapter Four
   "G Forces" 21

Chapter Five
   Edging the P.O. 25

Chapter Six
   What Was Old is New Again 29

Chapter Seven
   It's Not How You Lick It, It's Where You Stick It! 33

Chapter Eight
   Back to the Future! 39

Chapter Nine
   Old Rate, New Rate, How do You Rate? 43

Chapter Ten
   Metered Mail 49
Chapter Eleven
   Ethics 53
Chapter Twelve
   What to do if you get Caught! 59
Conclusion 63

Introduction

Practice makes perfect! Work hard and do a good job and you will go places! It costs 33¢ to mail a first class letter! What do these phrases have in common? They are all myths that we have been duped into believing.

Practice may make you better at something, but without the natural talent or aptitude, no amount of practice will make you perfect! Working hard and doing a good job will make you tired and old, as the people who "brown nose" go places you only dream of.

As for needing 33¢ to mail a first class letter, you can mail one for a whole lot less than that, and sometimes for nothing at all!

On January 1, 1995, the Postal Service got their long anticipated rate hike from 29¢ to 32¢ for first class postage. On December 31, 1994, the local Postmaster was being interviewed on the 6:00 news. He said that the Post Office would run late processing the mail to make sure that people who had mailed letters with only 29¢ postage, would get them postmarked before the rate hike went into effect at midnight.

The Post Office was processing more mail than normal. It seems everybody and their dog was paying their bills and getting all correspondence taken care of before the price of mailing went up. The Post Office was swamped by the last minute rush. With the cost of postage hours away from going up, the Post Office was experiencing an increase in sales and usage of their main product, the First Class Stamp! From a purely marketing standpoint, someone at the Postal Service deserved credit for being a genius!

The interviewer asked the Postmaster what would happen if someone tried to mail a letter with only a 29¢ stamp after the deadline. The Postmaster said, "Some will get through, but the overwhelming majority will be sent back for additional postage." The Postmaster also said not to use 29¢ stamps to pay your utility bills, because the utility companies would not accept them without proper postage.

I looked at my friend Roy and said, "Did you catch that? He just used a scare tactic. What a bunch of bullshit propaganda!"

Roy asked, "Do you think he is making that up?"

"Of course!" I snapped back. "The Post Office is run by the Federal Government, and they have access to the best propaganda people in the business. They plant a lie in your mind and then use FEAR to build a wall around the lie so that you believe it. Once you believe the lie, you become a source of power for the propagandist using that lie."

"Aren't people too intelligent to be manipulated by propaganda?" Roy asked.

Introduction

"Most Americans will believe anything you tell them, if you are convincing enough, or in a position of authority that they respect and trust. Look at how many weekly tabloids are popular." I said. "You have to understand the difference between beliefs and knowledge. Do you know the difference?"

"I'm sure you're going to tell me," Roy said.

"Knowledge is truth and facts based on logical evaluations. A belief is a state of mind in which trust or confidence is placed in something without evidence or proof."

"Well," Roy said. "Do something about it then!" A smile crossed his lips. He had just challenged me to take action by gathering the facts and spreading the word.

I have one rule I live by. Never believe anything without thoroughly checking the facts. The fact is, most people are too afraid to challenge the Government, City Hall, the School District, the IRS, or the Postal Service. And that fear is a powerful weapon used in advertising and propaganda!

On January 2, 1995, I obtained permission from a local utility company to root through the envelopes in the mailroom garbage. The results were both astounding and shocking. This led me to experiment on my own, to probe the chinks in the postal armor. The findings of this research are contained in the following pages.

You can fool all of the people some of the time. And you can fool some of the people all of the time. But you can't fool all of the people all of the time. It was only a matter of time before they were found out!

Chapter One
"Technology is Our Friend"

Cut your postage costs in half! Mail first class letters for only 2¢ each! Mail some letters absolutely free! Sound too good to be true? Well, it is true. Scientific research has proven that all of this is possible.

By thoroughly gathering the facts and documenting the evidence, I have identified numerous ways to do all of that and more. But how is all of this possible, you might ask? I'll tell you in one word. TECHNOLOGY.

Technology is our friend! In the old days, letters had to be hand-canceled, shipped by truck, train, or plane, to be delivered. Today, the Post Office handles literally millions of pieces of mail each day. Using the old methods would take too long and cost more, because the Post Office would have to hire more people just to sort and cancel letters.

Enter technology and automation. The Postal Service has spent five billion dollars to install Optical Character Readers (OCRs), and Bar Code Sorters (BCSs), in most sorting operations in the United States. These computerized mail processing techno wonders increase the speed, efficiency, and accuracy of processing mail. At ten pieces of mail per second, they "read" and sort 36,000 pieces of mail per hour. Wow!

The Optical Character Reader scans the delivery address and then prints a bar code at the bottom of the letter, which represents the ZIP code for that address. Then, the bar code scanner reads only the bar code before sending the letter to the proper channel for delivery. These machines also look for and cancel the stamp on the envelope.

As you can see from this, most pieces of mail move through the Post Office without a human being ever looking to see if there was a stamp on any of them. If the machines do not detect a stamp, they will reject that letter, and then a postal worker will become aware of it.

Is there any way to beat these techno wonders, you might ask? YES! They are only machines that are run by computers. These computers only do what they have been programmed to do by humans. They cannot think like a human can. So, if you know what to do, you can out think them. But to do that, you have to know their weaknesses and limitations.

The first weakness is speed. At 36,000 pieces of mail per hour, some errors can occur in sorting and delivery. About one in every thousand pieces of mail will make it through the sorter without a stamp on it. One out of fifty will go through so fast that it won't even get postmarked!

The second weakness is that the machines are colorblind! Stamps are printed with a phosphorescent coating on them. The machines look for that and then cancel it. It is possible to fool the machines with things that have a similar coating. They cancel the envelope and send it on its way.

The third weakness is the bar code. Even without a stamp on it, if a bar code was preprinted on the envelope, the BCSs often send them on their way with a cancellation mark over the area of the envelope that says "Place Stamp Here."

The fourth weakness is that the machines don't know math. They cannot recognize a 2¢ stamp from a 33¢ stamp. Some people have taken advantage of this to mail first class mail for 2¢ each! Even if your letter must be sent to the proper delivery channel by an employee-operated address checker, they are not likely to notice that the postage is improper. They are trained to look at the address and send it on its way. They are not trained to look at the stamp.

The fifth weakness is that the machines can only read typewritten addresses. If you hand print or hand write the address, the sorter will kick your letter out to be sorted and canceled by a postal employee. But preprinted return envelopes from utility companies and other businesses, often have the bar code printed on the envelope already. The OCRs and BCSs can process them for hours.

To test the techniques that will be discussed in the rest of this book, we used Billings, Montana as our test site. There are two reasons for that. First, Billings, Montana, is a typical medium-sized city of 93,000 people, whose Post Office had been using the sorting machines for about two years. Second, Billings is a consistent top performer in recent surveys for on-time delivery of first class mail. They usually rank in the top three in the nation.

I was able to talk a local utility company into letting me dig through the envelopes in the mailroom garbage. I made some astounding observations, which led to test mailings to confirm or disprove the theories that I began to formulate. The results and documented proof fill the rest of this book.

Figure 1-1 shows three envelopes that were postmarked without a stamp on them at all. The one at the top was cancelled on June 7, 1995. The second one was canceled August 3, 1995. The third was canceled August 22, 1995. Under that is a sticker that clearly states that it is not valid postage. Yet it was canceled on June 22, 1995. And last is a sticker from a veteran's organization that looks like a stamp because of the flag on it. It isn't a stamp, though; it is a sticker yet it was canceled on August 16, 1995.

Chapter One
"Technology is Our Friend"
9

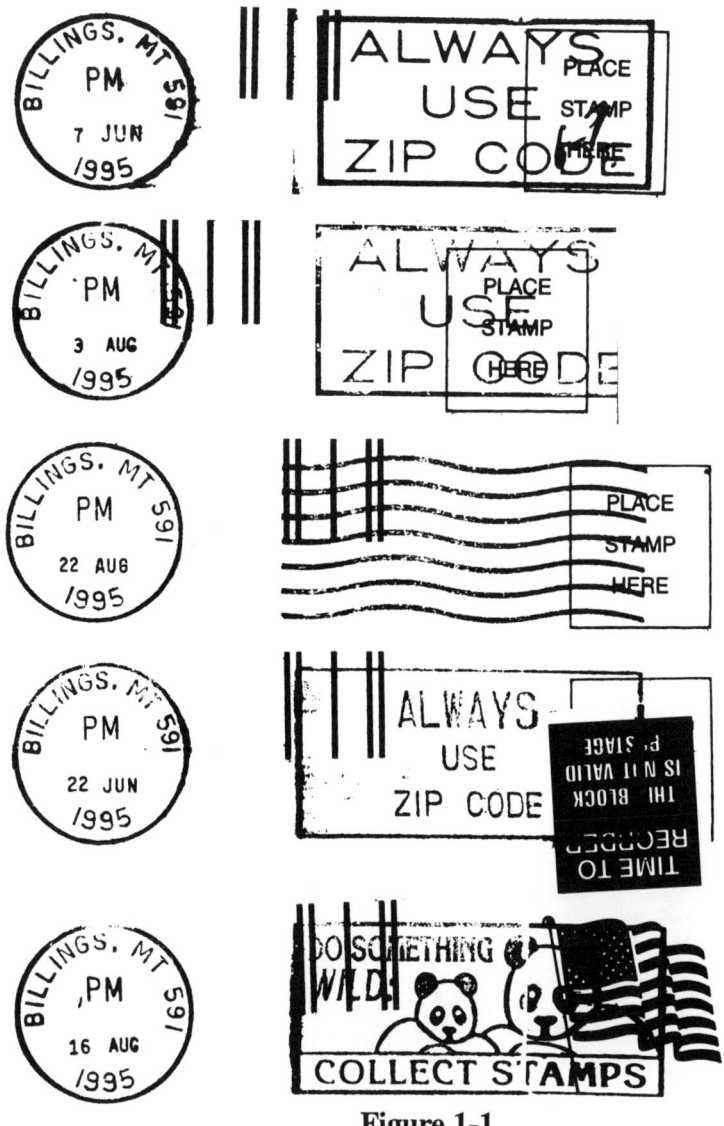

Figure 1-1

Chapter Two
Cut Your Postage Rates in Half

The first technique I will discuss is how to cut your postage rates in half, literally. My friend Roy and I were sifting through the mailroom garbage at a local utility company. We were looking for evidence that someone had successfully mailed a letter with a 29¢ stamp after the January 1, 1995, deadline.

Most of the letters had a combination of a 29¢ stamp, and a 3¢ stamp of some sort. Some of the 29¢ stamps were the large commemoratives. They are about twice the size of an ordinary stamp.

Roy said, "Look at this big stamp, the cancellation mark is only on the top half."

I looked at it and said, "You're right." Then I grinned and continued looking for the elusive lone 29¢ stamped envelope.

"It's too bad you can't cut the top part off and use the bottom half," Roy continued. "The bottom half looks new yet!"

I looked up from the pile of letters. "Why don't we cut it off and try it?" I asked.

So, the top part of the stamp with the cancellation mark was removed. The lower half was glued onto an envelope that I then mailed back to my own address. It looked kind of funny because it didn't even have a value printed on it. The value was on the top part that was cut off.

The next day when the mail arrived, lo and behold, there was our letter with only half a stamp. A cancellation mark was on it. There was no postage due notice. Only the letter with half a stamp.

I grinned and showed it to Roy. "What do you make of that?"

"You gotta love those commemoratives," he said.

Figure 2-1 shows how a 32¢ commemorative stamp looks after the good part is cut away from the part with the cancellation mark on it. I advise that you use the portion with the value on it for best success. However, in the middle is the bottom part that I mailed to myself with no value on it. It is postmarked January 9, 1995. At the bottom, half of a commemorative is used with a "G" Rate make-up stamp, which has a value of 3¢. It is postmarked January 27, 1995. Total cost of mailing it was 3¢.

Chapter Two
Cut Your Postage Rates in Half

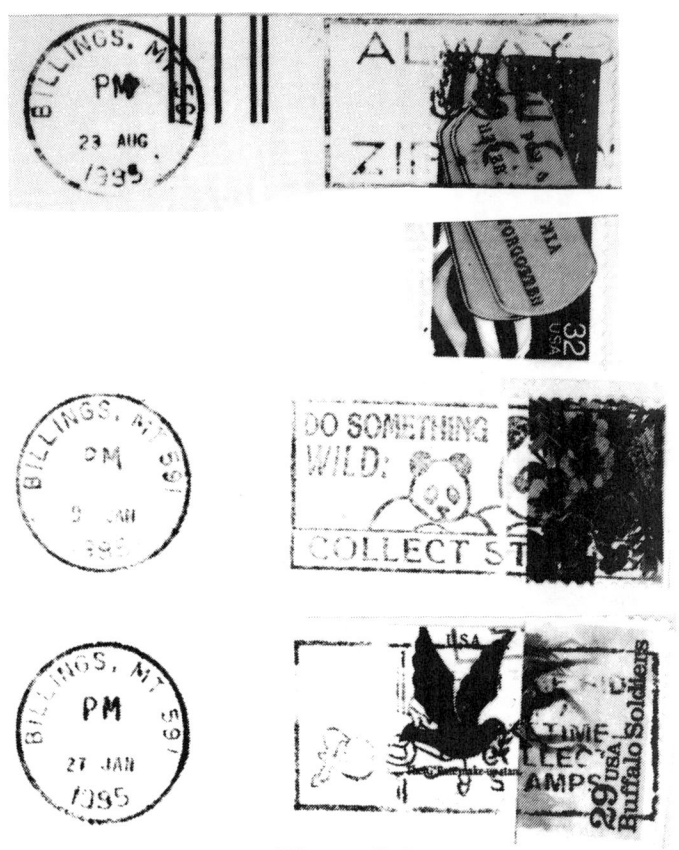

Figure 2-1

Figure 2-2 shows four halves of commemoratives that were used. The second one again didn't show a value. The top one was postmarked August 14, 1995. The second one was postmarked August 16, 1995. The Marilyn Monroe half stamp was postmarked August 18, 1995. The half United Nations one was postmarked August 22, 1995.

How to Screw the Post Office

14

Figure 2-2

Chapter Two
Cut Your Postage Rates in Half
15

Figure 2-3 shows how I was able to take two stamps that had been canceled at an angle, but on different parts of the stamps. I cut them along the lines, and taped the good parts together to make one good stamp out of it! On the left is the finished good stamp. On the right are the two pieces left over.

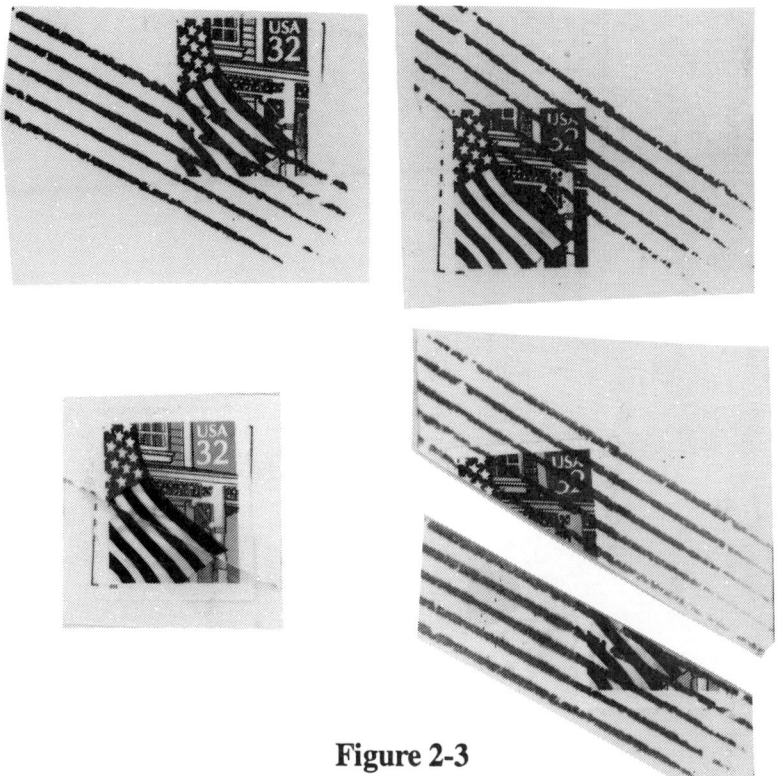

Figure 2-3

So, as you can see, you really can cut your postage rates in half. If you buy a commemorative stamp, cut it in half right away. Use one half on one letter, and the other half on another letter. Experiment for yourself to see what works best for you.

Chapter Three
2¢ Makes Sense

My friend Roy ran a mail order business a few years ago. He kept getting information through the mail that said he could mail all his first class letters for only 2¢ each. Indeed, each offer of this information asked him to check the envelope it arrived in, as it had arrived with only a 2¢ stamp on it.

Roy threw the first bunch of them away. They always wanted five dollars for this powerful secret. He didn't pay the five bucks. Remembering this, I went to talk to the local postmaster.

He laughed at me and said, "No, you can't do that!" "There used to be a postal regulation that allowed that under certain circumstances, but it's obsolete," he said.

"How did it work?" I asked.

"It was simple," he said. "All you had to do was put a 2¢ stamp on the envelope. Then, the words "FIRST CLASS" were printed next to, or under the stamp, and in the lower left corner of the envelope using a rubber stamp."

"But you can't do that anymore?" I asked.

"No. As I said, that regulation was obsolete long ago, back when a regular stamp cost only 5¢."

I thanked him for his time and left. When I got home, I immediately addressed a letter to myself and put a 2¢ stamp on it. Then I went to a local print shop and bought a rubber stamp that said "FIRST CLASS." I stamped the envelope in the corners with "FIRST CLASS," as the postmaster had told me. Then I mailed it.

Roy said, "I thought the guy at the Post Office said that was illegal."

"No he didn't," I said. "He told me it was obsolete! He only wanted me to believe it was illegal."

"Oh, I see, a technicality!" Roy said.

"Exactly," I replied. More propaganda. It's still in the postal regulations, but it is outdated! Kind of the same way that most states still have laws that oral sex is illegal. Those laws are obsolete, but nobody ever took them off the books.

Furthermore, I knew that the OCRs didn't know the difference between a 2¢ or a 32¢ stamp. Also, the cent symbol, "¢" disappeared from postage stamps in the early 1980's. The postal service spokesman said it was for aesthetic reasons.

This caused some people to believe that they were dollar stamps if it were a single-digit value. So a 2¢ stamp was often confused for a $2.00 stamp, even by postal employees. However, as of this writing, the postal service has changed that. From now on, all low value stamps will have a cent symbol to clearly designate the value.

Chapter Three
2¢ Makes Sense
19

But, don't let that stop you. As I said earlier, the OCRs can't tell a 2¢ stamp from a 33¢ stamp.

The next day after I mailed myself a letter with a 2¢ stamp, it arrived. Was there "postage due" you might ask? Absolutely not.

So, as you can see, using a 2¢ stamp is even better than cutting your postage in half.

Figure 3-1 shows the same 2¢ stamped envelope I mailed to myself. It is postmarked January 9, 1995. Under the postage stamp is the rubber stamped "FIRST CLASS MAIL." The second one is one of the offers that Roy got. It was postmarked from Honolulu on April 25, 1994. Next to the postage stamp is the rubber stamped "FIRST CLASS MAIL."

Figure 3-1

Chapter Four

"G Forces"

When the Post Office gets a rate increase, it usually is not certain it will get the increase it asked for. That is determined by the Postal Rate Commission. Until they are certain, they cannot print stamps with the new value on them. So they have a contingency stamp.

They print stamps with a letter of the alphabet on them. The first was the "A" stamp. The most recent in the order have been the "G" and "H" stamps. My early research dealt with the "G" stamps, so they will be discussed in detail in this chapter.

"G" stamps came in a variety of styles and colors. Depending on whether they were in a sheet of fifty, a sheet of 100, a roll of 100, a book of stamps, or peel and stick. Also, a yellow version was printed for postcard use, and a blue version for presorted mail.

Regular "G" stamp value is 32¢. The postcard "G" stamp value is 20¢, and the presort "G" stamp value is 23¢. This was one of the observations I made while going through the mailroom trash at the utility company. Either by mistake, or on purpose, some people used the "G" postcard stamp, and a few used the "G" presort stamp, instead of the 32¢ value regular "G" stamp.

The OCR, not knowing the difference, cancelled them and sent them on their way. What this means, is that some people saved 12¢ off the postage cost by using a postcard stamp, and some saved 9¢ by using a presort stamp. That's a nice discount.

Even though the postcard "G" stamp is yellow, and the presort "G" stamp is blue, the letter carrier had not noticed. And no wonder. They are trained to look for the address so they can make the delivery. Looking at the stamp is secondary. And with a large volume of mail, this is seldom noticed!

Also, when the 32¢ rate hike came into effect, there was an immediate shortage of 3¢ stamps to make up the difference for the rather abundant 29¢ stamps still in existence. For this, the Postal Service also had a contingency stamp. Called the "G" rate make-up stamp, it was printed with a bluebird on it. Its value was 3¢, and was to accompany a 29¢ stamp to equal the 32¢ rate.

For some people, it became the "Blue Bird of Happiness!" Dozens of letters were found that had only the "Bluebird" stamp on them. Once again, the OCRs didn't know the difference, and canceled them and sent them on their way!

This was a savings of 29¢ per letter. How's that for a discount? So, as you can see, you really can save money on your postage by letting the "G" force be with you.

Chapter Four
"G Forces"
23

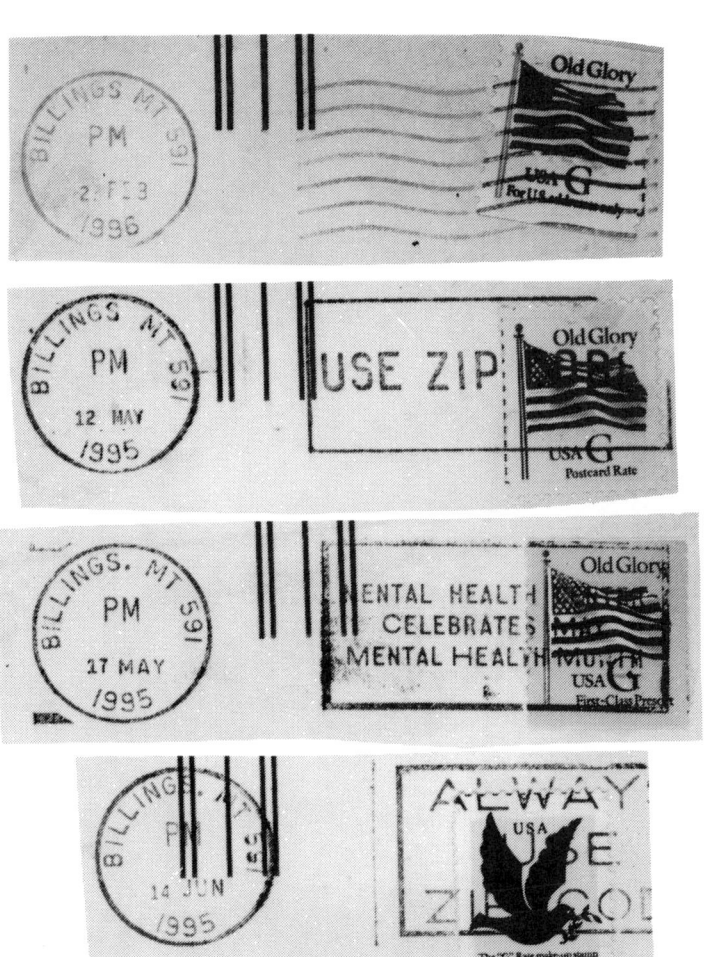

Figure 4-1

Figure 4-1 shows a regular "G" stamp at the top. Under it, is a "G" postcard rate stamp, postmarked May 12, 1995. Third is a "G" first-class presort stamp, postmarked May 17, 1995. And last is a "Bluebird" "G" rate make-up stamp, postmarked June 14, 1995.

Chapter Five
Edging the P.O.

And now, for my next trick, I will show you one way to mail a first class letter with no postage at all! I conceived of the idea when my friend last actually bought a sheet of stamps.

I don't know if you have ever paid attention to a sheet of stamps, so I'll elaborate. Besides the printed postage stamps, there is a peripheral edge on all four sides of the sheet of stamps. Some of the edges are at least as wide as a stamp. Some of the edge has printing on it too, like "Use ZIP Code."

Stamps are printed with a special phosphorescent coating. This coating is recognized by the OCRs as a stamp, and the OCR prints a postmark on it and sends it on its way. It stands to reason that the entire sheet that the stamps are printed on is covered with this special coating. Even the edge!

I looked a Roy and said, "Save me the edges off your sheet of stamps, OK?"

"What are you up to now?" he asked. "I see that twinkle in your eye. Are you going to print your own stamps on it?"

"No," I said. "I thought I would mail a letter with just the blank edge." And so I did. You guessed it. The next day my self-addressed letter arrived with a postmark over the piece of peripheral edge from a sheet of stamps. In fact, several smaller pieces laid edge to edge to make the size of a stamp also worked.

Some of the new peel and stick sheets of stamps contain a corner the size of a stamp that works well, too. On it is printed the words, "TIME TO REORDER, THIS BLOCK IS NOT VALID POSTAGE." Since it is coated like the stamps are, the OCRs print a postmark on it and send it on its way!

To counter this, the Postal Service started perforating them so they will not go through the machines. The countermeasure that I use to counter this is to put a piece of Scotch tape across the middle of this block to hold it together. Be careful not to cover the entire block, as the OCR will not see the coating and will reject it. Leave the top and bottom uncovered.

So, as you can see, this is one edge in your favor when it comes to mailing your first class letters for free!

Figure 5-1 shows an edge from a sheet of stamps that is postmarked December 28, 1994. Second is one of the peel and stick reorder blocks, postmarked July 9, 1995.

Chapter Five
Edging the P.O.
27

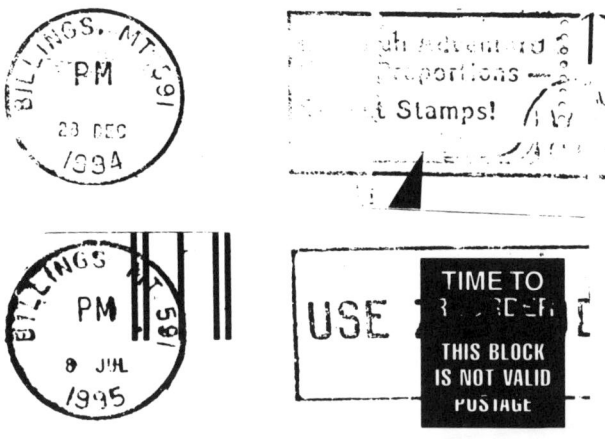

Figure 5-1

Chapter Six

What Was Old is New Again

One of the things that I noticed while going through the letters in the mailroom was the postmark. They also come in a variety of styles. The old-fashioned wavy lines we're all used to, and new ones that have animals on them and encourage you to collect stamps. I would encourage you to collect stamps too!

Some of the postmarks cover only a portion of the stamp. Some go across the top of the stamp and leave the rest untouched. Some cover the whole stamp, but if the ink was running out, they left only a very light postmark, which is barely noticeable!

Most of the stamps with a very light postmark will pass through the OCRs like a new stamp. Very carefully peel the envelope off the stamp, not the stamp off the envelope. This will result in the stamp usually being left intact, but without mucilage, the sticky stuff you normally lick on the back of the stamps. Or you may want to soak the stamps off the paper by placing them in a bowl of hot water. Just use some white glue to affix it to your next first class letter and you're good to go.

For stamps with a black mark on only one edge, just cut the bad part off. Then reuse the good portion on a letter. If too much of the stamp has to be cut off, be creative. Look for stamps of the same type that are postmarked on the other edge of the stamp. That way, when the bad parts are cut off, you are left with two good parts, which if laid side by side look and act as a new stamp. A good example of this can be seen in Chapter Two, Figure 2-3.

This same technique can be used for stamps that are postmarked across the top on one, and the bottom of another. Here again, the stamp must be of the same type.

And what about stamps that have a heavy post mark on them? I suggest you experiment in your area. In the tests I ran, even stamps with a heavy postmark went right through the OCRs without a hitch!

These four techniques, used to your advantage, give you four more ways to mail your first class letters for free. To the OCRs, what was old is new again!

Figure 6-1 shows a "G" stamp with the postmark catching only the left edge. That edge could be cut off, leaving most of the stamp to be used again. Below it is an example of a wavy postmark that caught only the very top of these stamps. Again, it could be cut off, leaving most of the stamps to be reused again.

Chapter Six
What Was Old is New Again
31

Figure 6-1

Figure 6-2 shows five different postmarked stamps. If you look carefully at them, you will see that each of them has at least two different postmarkings on them. This would indicate that even though they were already used, somebody reused them with success anyway!

How to Screw the Post Office

32

Figure 6-2

Chapter Seven

It's Not How You Lick It, It's Where You Stick It!

For this one, I think it is helpful to have the cooperation of someone that you correspond with regularly. It has to do with the placement of the stamps on the envelope.

When the envelope passes through the OCR, a cancellation mark is usually made across the upper right corner of the envelope. This is where the stamp is supposed to be. But what happens if the stamp is placed lower than normal? The cancellation mark hits the envelope in the upper right corner and misses the stamp. Or maybe it hits only part of the stamp. The stamp can then be removed and used again.

This is why I suggest you have the cooperation of a close friend or relative that you regularly correspond with. Otherwise, the person receiving the letter will probably throw away the envelope, and a reusable stamp with it.

Another method is to use two stamps. Let's say a 29¢ stamp and a 3¢ stamp to make the 32¢ rate. Place the 3¢ stamp in the upper right corner where it belongs. Place the 29¢ stamp below the 3¢ stamp. This way the 3¢ stamp gets canceled and the 29¢ stamp is unscathed and still reusable!

Sometimes you can get the same results by placing them side by side with the 3¢ stamp in the corner. However, from observations, I would suggest the top and bottom configuration!

If you are using a large commemorative stamp, and the value is at the top, place the stamp on the envelope upside down. This will cause the cancellation mark to go across the bottom of the stamp. Now your friend on the receiving end can cut the stamp in half and use the part with the value of it as a regular stamp as discussed in Chapter Two.

If the commemorative has the value at the bottom, place the stamp where it belongs, but slightly lower than normal. This will cause the cancellation mark to hit only the extreme upper part of the stamp. Again, the person on the receiving end can now cut the stamp in half and use the part with the value on it as a regular stamp!

It should go without saying that you should always be on the lookout on the mail you receive to see how many stamps you can reuse.

Figure 7-1 shows three groups of stamps as they were recovered from used envelopes. In the top one, four stamps were used to make the value of 32¢. The top two 10¢ stamps were cancelled. The bottom 10¢ and 2¢ stamps were not even close too being hit. In the second one, the 29¢ stamp got the cancellation mark, and the Bluebird took a wavy line across the very top. In this one, it would have been better if the Bluebird had been on top. In the third set,

Chapter Seven
It's Not How You Lick It, It's Where You Stick It!
35

two 23¢ stamps were used. The top one got the cancellation mark and the bottom one was untouched.

Figure 7-1

36

Figure 7-2 shows three groups of stamps as they were recovered from used envelopes. In the first set, seven stamps were used to make the 32¢ rate. The fourth stamp out from the upper right corner was untouched, as were the three 4¢ stamps on the bottom.

Figure 7-2

Chapter Seven
It's Not How You Lick It, It's Where You Stick It!

In the second set, four stamps were used and they all got hit by the cancellation mark. The 1¢ stamp may be salvageable if the bird's head is cut off. This is a good example as to why a top to bottom configuration is preferred. In the third set, three stamps were used to make the 32¢ rate. The 5¢ stamp has minimal damage from the cancellation mark. It took a mild hit on both sides. Again, I would trim that part off and reuse it.

Chapter Eight
Back to the Future!

I call this method Back to the Future! It is one more way to mail first class letters for free! Before I tell you what it is, I need to explain the mechanics of a first class envelope.

In the upper right hand corner of the envelope is the place where a first class postage stamp is supposed to go. In the upper left corner is the return address (your address if you are the one sending the letter). In the center right, is the forwarding address, or the addressee. That is the person the letter is being sent to. That is how a normal first class envelope should look!

I actually stumbled onto this idea by accident. I was trying to mail a letter to my sister without using a stamp. The next day, my letter came back to me with a note stamped on it by the Post Office that said "RETURNED FOR POSTAGE."

I thought about that for a second. Then I addressed another envelope. This time, I put my sister's address in the area where the return address should go. I put my address where the addressee should go. And again, I mailed it without a stamp.

The next day, my sister called me on the phone. She got the letter with the reversed address. Again it was stamped by the Post Office, "RETURNED FOR POSTAGE." My sister was a little confused because she knew she hadn't mailed it. I told her what I was testing, and that the letter was for her.

Inside, I had put a return envelope for her to mail her letter to me, also with the reversed address. She wouldn't use it, but she did save the envelope I had sent her. I still have it.

I asked her if the mailman made her pay the postage on it before he would give it to her. She said no, and added that she didn't think that what I had done was very ethical. More on that later!

As you can see, reverse addressing is a method of sending first class letters for free. I suggest that you experiment to see if it works for you!

Chapter Eight
Back to the Future!

Joe Smith
1111 No Street
Anytown, USA

Stamp

Al Smith
1212 No Avenue
No City, USA

Chapter Nine

Old Rate, New Rate, How do You Rate?

As I rooted through the mailroom garbage at the utility company looking for the proof I needed, a feeling of excitement came over me. I was about to make a series of discoveries. I did not have to wait long.

There it was! The single 29¢ stamp on an envelope that was postmarked after January 1, 1995. Proof positive that a 29¢ stamp could be used yet. And found at a utility company after the Postmaster said that utility companies would not accept them. But was it a single sample that had accidentally slipped through? Only further digging in the trash would tell for sure.

Surprise! There was a second, then a third. All together there were fourteen envelopes that had made it with only 29¢ postage. That was about one out of every fifty that had arrived with only a 29¢ stamp.

How to Screw the Post Office

That was not the only discovery, though! A few people had used a single 19¢ stamp, meant to be used on a post card. Amazingly, they had made it through without detection. I also found envelopes that had 25¢, 23¢, 20¢, 3¢, and 1¢ stamps. There were no postage due notices on any of them.

There was yet another thing that I observed. Fourteen envelopes had stamps on them, but no postmark! They had gone through the sorting machine so fast, that it totally missed them.

The main purpose of my dig through the mailroom trash was to find envelopes that had been postmarked after January 1, 1995, which had less than 32¢ postage. I was not disappointed. Over the next couple of weeks, I consistently found the same things.

I now knew that envelopes with less than 32¢ postage were going undetected. So you can really put any stamp on your letter, and it has an excellent chance of passing undetected. See the examples, illustrations 9-1 through 9-3.

Figure 9-1 shows a 32¢ stamp postmarked on January 23, 1996, at the top. Below it is a 29¢ stamp postmarked January 24, 1996. In the center is a 29¢ stamp postmarked August 14, 1995. Fourth, is a 29¢ stamp postmarked January 24, 1995. And last is a 32¢ stamp postmarked January 23, 1996. This was done so that you can see that the postmarks are not phony. They are consistent and from the same source.

Chapter Nine
Old Rate, New Rate, How do You Rate?
45

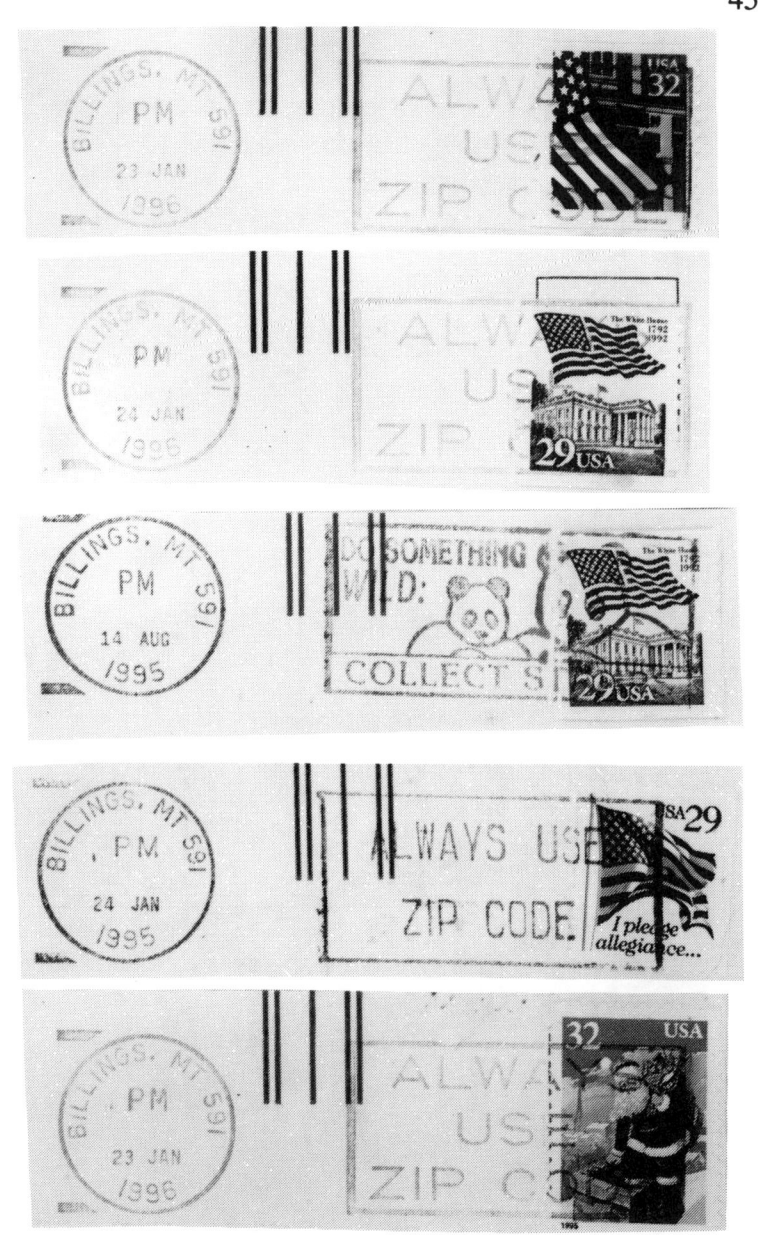

Figure 9-1

46

Figure 9-2 shows a 19¢ stamp postmarked January 6, 1995. Below it is a 20¢ stamp postmarked July 14, 1995. Third is a 23¢ stamp postmarked June 5, 1995. And last is a 25¢ stamp with a postmark July 7, 1995.

Figure 9-2

Chapter Nine
Old Rate, New Rate, How do You Rate?
47

Figure 9-3 shows a 1¢ stamp at the top, postmarked March 14, 1995. In the middle is a 3¢ stamp postmarked January 10, 1995. Last is a 3¢ stamp postmarked February 17, 1995.

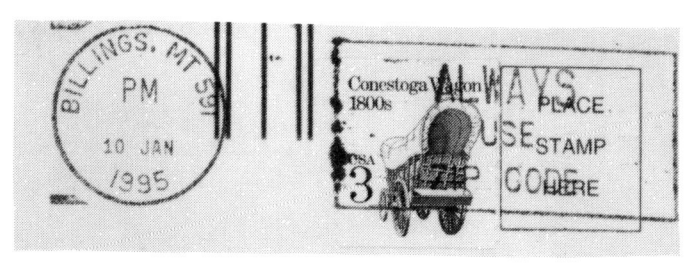

Figure 9-3

Chapter Ten

Metered Mail

One of the observations that I made while examining the envelopes in the mailroom had to do with metered mail. For those of you not familiar with metered mail, I'll explain.

Metered mail has the value of the postage printed directly on the envelope by a postage meter. Pitney Bowes is the largest manufacturer of postage meters. Businesses use them for their convenience of speed in printing the postage rate on envelopes versus putting stamps on the envelopes. Also, non-profit organizations and bulk mailers can print a lower rate on the envelope, depending on what their permit allows them to do.

The Pitney Bowes meter machine keeps track of the dollar amount of postage printed by that meter. When a preset value has been used up, the meter user has to have the meter reset, and pay for either the postage printed, or a designated sum in advance to be printed later.

Metered mail almost never gets a cancellation mark from the Post Office. The postage meter prints the postmark and the value at the same time. But because the ink is not phosphorescent, the OCRs kick them out and a postal worker has to handle them.

Since they weren't canceled by an OCR, I cut some off and glued them to envelopes to see what would happen if I mailed them. Some of them made it, and some of them did not. If you are going to try using this method, I recommend that you also glue at least a piece of a stamp, or the edge from a sheet of stamps, on the envelope as well. That way, the OCRs will be less likely to kick it out.

Figure 10-1 shows three examples of metered mail. The top one is funny to me, because there is no value printed on it. I am the only one who noticed it. So if you do get a meter machine for yourself, set the value for 0.00. The second one shows a value of 29¢ on January 4, 1995. It should have been 32¢. The third one is one that I successfully cut, glued, and mailed to myself. It was postmarked January 27, 1995.

*Chapter Ten
Metered Mail*
51

Figure 10-1

Chapter Eleven
Ethics

My sister, my good friend Roy, and a few others, all think that beating the Post Office is unethical. My sister said that although she thought it was funny, she did not approve of it. My sister said that she would continue to pay whatever price for her postage because it was the "Christian thing to do."

And my good friend Roy said that you are not only paying for a stamp, you are paying for a service. The service of delivering your letter to wherever it goes in a timely manner. To use the service and not pay for it is just not right.

My answer to them is simply this. The Postal Service isn't ethical on all counts either. Is it ethical for the Postmaster to go on the evening news and knowingly lie to everyone? Telling people that the utility companies would not accept your bill payments unless there was proper postage on the envelope. My observations proved that to be bullshit!

In my opinion, the Postal Propagandists are anything but ethical. They had some people so afraid that their bills

How to Screw the Post Office

would not be paid, that they overpaid on the postage. Some people used two 29¢ stamps for lack of 3¢ stamps to make up the rate difference. These people overpaid on the service they received. They did not get a refund. And I can assure you that from my observations, there were no shortage of those that overpaid! More people overpaid than underpaid.

And on top of that, there was a shortage of 3¢ stamps, and 3¢ make-up stamps. This caused another phenomenon besides doubling up on the 29¢ stamps. Some people used ancient postage from their stamp collections to make up the difference. Some of these stamps were fifty years old, and worth more than the cost of first class postage to be sure.

Is it ethical to cause a shortage of the 3¢ stamps necessary to make the difference? This forced some people to decide between using more postage than was necessary, or using valuable stamps from collections to make sure that their bills got paid.

And what about the service you do get? I can't count how many times I have found mail in my box that belonged to a neighbor, or in some instances a person who lives six blocks away from me! The Post Office takes off numerous holidays, causing you to go without service at all on those days. We are captive customers, like it or not.

So, don't feel bad about getting one over on the Post Office. They aren't angels either, and they feel no remorse about price increases or using fear in their propaganda.

When I was testing used stamps on envelopes that I had addressed to myself, one came with a postmark that said, "DO SOMETHING WILD, COLLECT STAMPS." I showed it to Roy and said, "You see, the Postal Service encourages me to do something wild!"

Chapter Eleven
Ethics
55

I encourage you to do something wild and use the techniques in this book.

Figure 11-1 shows six 29¢ stamps clearly postmarked after January 1, 1995 when the rate should have been 32¢. So it was, and is possible to use the old stamps for postage, and that's all there is to it.

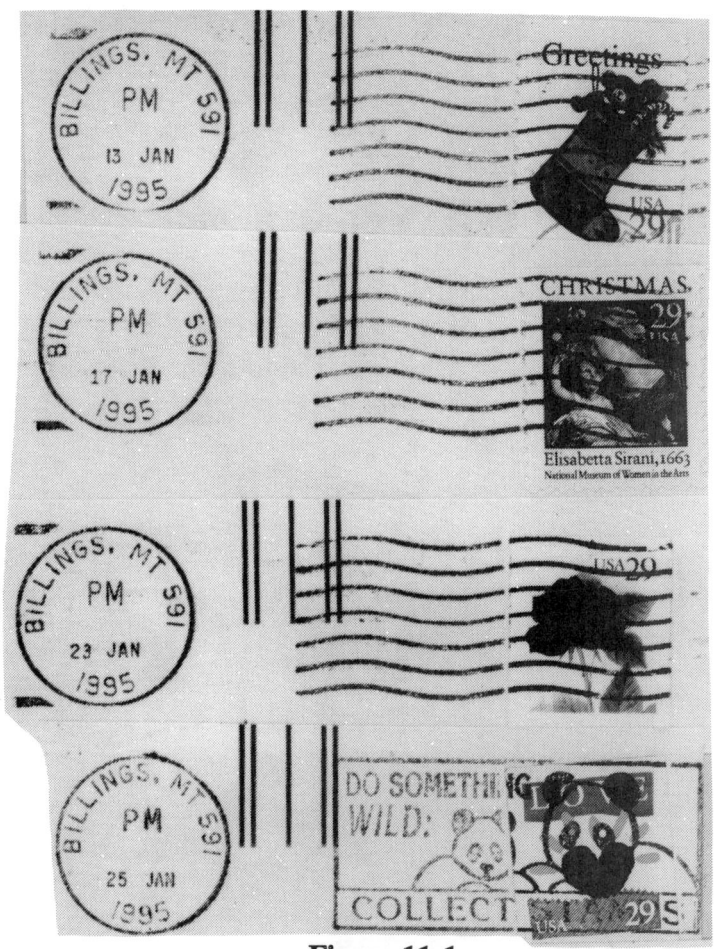

Figure 11-1

How to Screw the Post Office

Figure 11-1 (Continued)

Figure 11-2 shows five cases of overpayment of postage. The top two show that two 29¢ stamps were used. The middle one shows the use of a 52¢ stamp. The fourth one shows the use of a 29¢ stamp, and a "G" rate stamp worth 32¢, for a total of 61¢ postage. The fifth one shows a 32¢ value "G" stamp, and a Bluebird stamp worth 3¢. The Bluebird stamp was not needed.

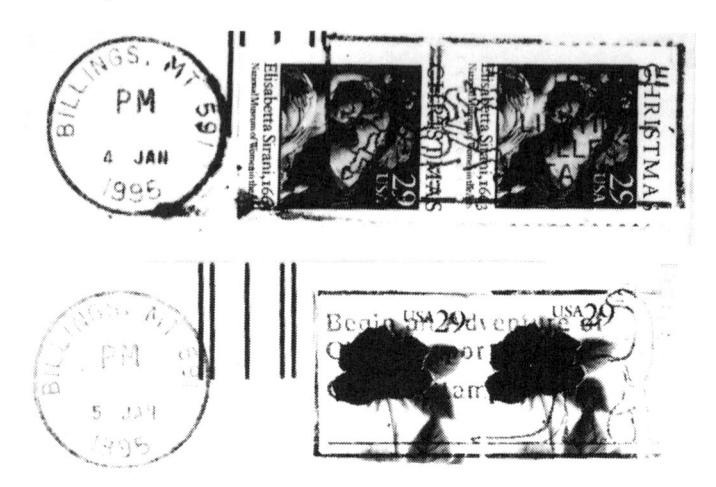

Figure 11-2

Chapter Eleven
Ethics
57

Figure 11-2 (Continued)

Figure 11-3 shows two cases where old stamps from collections were used. In the top one a 22¢ stamp was used with a 10¢ stamp to make the 32¢ rate. The second one shows an old 1957 3¢ stamp used with a 29¢ stamp.

Figure 11-3

Chapter Twelve

What to do if you get Caught!

OK. Let's say you've been using the techniques in this book to beat the high cost of mailing first class letters. And let's say that you have experimented in your area to see which ones work best for you. Part of the experimentation process is also finding out which techniques do not work well where you live.

That means there is every possibility that a postman may end up on your doorstep to collect postage due. Or it means your letters might be sent back to you for postage, or additional postage. What do you do when this happens? That's what this chapter is all about. What to do if you get caught cheating!

RULE #1: PLAY DUMB. It can be real embarrassing to have a letter carrier standing in front of you telling you that you can't mail letters for only 2¢. That happened to me on one occasion.

I gave my best dumb look of confusion and thanked him for returning them to me. Then I waited a few days and mailed them again. The second time they went through.

On another occasion a letter carrier needed 32¢ postage due before I could get my letter and see what had not worked. I smiled and paid her the 32¢ and she left without a hassle.

RULE #2: PRETEND IT WAS A MISTAKE. The main thing is to never admit to doing anything wrong. I learned that from the Government! Presidents use this one and get away with it! If you don't confess your guilt, then the burden of proof lies with them. And it really is more likely in today's fast-paced lives that it was a simple mistake. Like when you send the check to the electric company, but you forgot to sign the check!

Like the example of using a 2¢ stamp and having it returned. Until recently, low denomination stamps didn't have the cent symbol. So a 2¢ stamp only said "2." It was easy to mistake it for a 2-dollar stamp. Even some postal employees made that mistake!

RULE #3: SMILE AND THANK THEM FOR POINTING OUT ANY ERROR. The postal service actually pays a company to test their accuracy. The program is called "The External First Class Mail Measurement System." It is run by the accounting firm Price Waterhouse. Testing is anonymously conducted during the course of the year.

Every day, Price Waterhouse places letters, flats and post cards in the mail around the nation. These are destined for people who are paid to monitor the service of the mail. The integrity of the system is very tight. Postal employees never

Chapter Twelve
What to do if you get Caught!

know which pieces of mail are part of a test, or who is monitoring them.

There is every possibility that you are paid by Price Waterhouse to test them. The Postal employees will usually be very polite when and if they point out an error to you. They want to score well if it was a test by Price Waterhouse.

So the possibility of being hauled off in chains and thrown in a damp dungeon is very slim. During testing, I only had three letters returned to me as undeliverable because of a lack of postage!

A Postal Inspector contacted me once to inform me that intent to avoid postage is a violation of Title 18, United States Code, Section 1725, and carries a penalty of a $5,000 fine. He also said a copy of this regulation was attached to my warning letter. It wasn't. So I went to my local Post office and asked them for a copy.

They could not find it in their book of regulations where the inspector said it was. They told me that it was really a different regulation, but they couldn't find a copy of that in their regulation book either. Sounds like fear tactics and propaganda bullshit to me!

Conclusion

Contained in this book are numerous ways to mail first class letters for less that 33¢ each. I have seen them all work through scientific observation. I do not guarantee that they will all work for you, or that they will work all of the time.

The Postal Service is ever changing, and might fix some of these problems of theirs. I could suggest ways to fix them, but I'm not on their payroll. And the fix would only drive up the cost of mailing letters. So my suggestion to the Postal Service is to let this sleeping dog lie. So few people cheat that they are better off doing nothing to change that. Every year since 1995, they have earned at least a billion dollars profit.

My suggestion to you is to experiment to see what works for you in your area. Do something wild and beat the high cost of postage!

You Will Also Want To Read:

☐ **19146 Your Revenge Is In The Mail,** *by Keith Wade.* There are a lot of jerks in the world who need to be taught a lesson. The problem is, how to get to them without causing yourself a lot of trouble? The answer is in this book. More than 60 letters you can copy and use to get even. *Sold for side-splitting entertainment purposes only. 1988, 5½ x 8½, 168 pp, soft cover.* $12.95.

☐ **19106 Poison Pen Letters,** *by Keith Wade.* A complete guide to getting revenge through the mail. If you've had problems with people or organizations that seem too big to fight back against, this book is for you. Covers retaliation against individuals, corporations and even government agencies. Includes nearly 100 letters, along with tips on stationery, mailing, and how to keep from getting caught. Sold for informational purposes only. *1984, 5½ x 8½, 103 pp, soft cover.* $12.95.

☐ **40079 How To Steal Food From The Supermarket,** *by J. Andrew Anderson.* Written by a supermarket security guard, this book will give your budget a boost! Learn all the ins and outs of shoplifting success, including: do-it-yourself markdowns; scamming the scanner; how to dress for success; defeating store security; and much more, including the one mistake that trips up most shoplifters and the one item you must bring shoplifting with you. *This offer is not available in stores. 1992, 5½ x 8½, 63 pp, soft cover.* $10.00.

☐ **61163 Identity Theft: The Cybercrime of the Millennium,** *by John Q. Newman.* Your most valuable possession is what makes you *you* — your identity. What would happen if someone stole it? Each year, more than 500,000 Americans fall victim to identity theft, and that number is rising. In this comprehensive book, you will learn: how thieves use computer networks and other information sources to adopt, use, and subsequently ravage the identities of unsuspecting victims; what you can do to protect yourself from identity theft, and how to fight back effectively if you are one of the unlucky victims. *1999, 5½ x 8½, 106 pp, soft cover.* $12.00.

☐ **91085 Secrets Of A Super Hacker,** *by The Knightmare, with an introduction by Gareth Branwyn.* The most amazing book on computer hacking ever written! Step-by-step, illustrated, details on the techniques used by hackers to get at your data, including: Stealing passwords; Password lists; Social engineering; Reverse social engineering; Trojan horses; Viruses; And much more! The how-to text is highlighted with bare-knuckle tales of the Knightmare's hacks. No person concerned with computer security should miss this amazing manual on mayhem. *1994, 8½ x 11, 205 pp, illustrated, soft cover.* **$19.95.**

☐ **40084 How To Sneak Into The Movies,** *by Dan Zamudio.* The author has worked in several movie theaters and reveals all his tricks for sneaking into the movies, including: The four basic ways to get into the movies free; Believable lines you can lay on a suspicious usher; How to sneak in with a date without looking cheap; Props you can use to strengthen your ruse; How to sneak in a whole gang of people; What to do if you're caught; And many more other ways to lower your movie-going costs. Highlighted with true tales of sneaking into some of America's great movie palaces. If you're tired of being milked for box office duds, then lower your cost of movie-going — and your risk of getting stuck — by learning exactly *How To Sneak Into The Movies! 1995, 5½ x 8½, 64 pp, soft cover.* **$8.00.**

☐ **19206 Out Of Business: Force a Company, Business or Store to Close Its Doors... for Good!,** *by Dennis Fiery.* When filing a formal complaint, asking for your money back, and engaging in healthy competition just don't do the trick, you need to take serious action. This book arms you with 101 ways to derail, deflate and destroy your target business. And if you want to protect your own business, this book is the best insurance policy you'll ever buy. The author gives new meaning to the term "corporate downsizing" in this revenge treatise. Sold for informational and entertainment purposes only. *1999, 5½ x 8½, 298 pp, soft cover.* **$17.95.**

☐ **19212 21st Century Revenge: Down & Dirty Tactics for the Millennium, by Victor Santoro.** The bad news: Technology has made some classic revenge tactics obsolete. The good news: Technology has opened the door to a slew of modern revenge methods never before possible! Master Revenge writer Victor Santoro explains how to turn technology to your advantage in the art of revenge. In this book you will learn: how to protect yourself from caller ID — and how to make it work for you; how to turn political correctness into political chaos; why your target's garbage can be his undoing; how the Internet is your world-wide resource for revenge. This book not only shows you how to form the ultimate revenge plan, but also how to protect yourself from those seeking revenge on you! *Sold for informational purposes only. 1999, 5½ x 8½, 150 pp, illustrated, soft cover. $15.00.*

---

*We offer the very finest in controversial and unusual books — a complete catalog is sent **FREE** with every book order. If you would like to order the catalog separately, please see our ad on the next page.*

SPO2

LOOMPANICS UNLIMITED
PO BOX 1197
PORT TOWNSEND, WA 98368

Please send me the books I have checked above. I am enclosing $ _____ which includes $4.95 for shipping and handling of orders up to $25.00. Add $1.00 for each additional $25.00 ordered *Washington residents please include 7.9% for sales tax.*

NAME_____

ADDRESS _____

CITY/STATE/ZIP_____

We accept Visa, Discover, and MasterCard. To place a credit card order *only,* call 1-800-380-2230, 24 hours a day, 7 days a week.

"Thank You very much for such prompt service. Keep it up with your wonderful titles, too. I believe this is the start of a wonderful business relationship." — J. Watt

"You guys are nuts... but I love it. My only problem is trying to figure out which books to order! Your catalog shouts freedom. Keep it up." — Biff

"Best catalog on the planet." — S. Scully

"Keep up the good work. I don't buy as much as I'd like to from you (just don't have time to read everything I'd like) but I enjoy the catalogs and the knowledge that you are there. Thanks." — Dave

"I've ordered from you for over ten years now. I did a search and found your web site on the Internet, so I thought I'd order some books. Let me say you've always been a great company to deal with and I am very satisfied with your company. Furthermore, your site is QUICK and EASY to access. Thanks!" — RMR

"Thanks for the info. When Lynnette introduced me to the catalogue, I thought that she was just freaky, but as I had a chance to peruse the info, I found myself falling in love with the catalogue. Thanks so much!" — Higgi the Great and Wonderful

"Thanks for the great books and service in the last twenty years!. — WC

THE BEST BOOK CATALOG IN THE WORLD!!!

We offer hard-to-find books on the world's most unusual subjects. Here are a few of the topics covered IN DEPTH in our exciting new catalog:

- *Hiding/Concealment of physical objects! A complete section of the best books ever written on hiding things.*
- *Fake ID/Alternate Identities! The most comprehensive selection of books on this little-known subject ever offered for sale! You have to see it to believe it!*
- *Investigative/Undercover methods and techniques! Professional secrets known only to a few, now revealed to you to use! Actual police manuals on shadowing and surveillance!*
- *And much, much more, including Locks and Lock Picking, Self-Defense, Intelligence Increase, Life Extension, Money-Making Opportunities, Human Oddities, Exotic Weapons, Sex, Drugs, Anarchism, and more!*

Our book catalog is over 200 pages, 8½ x 11, packed with more than 650 of the most controversial and unusual books ever printed! You can order every book listed! Periodic supplements keep you posted on the LATEST titles available!!! Our catalog is **$5.00**, including shipping and handling.

Our book catalog is truly THE BEST BOOK CATALOG IN THE WORLD! Order yours today. You will be very pleased, we know.

**LOOMPANICS UNLIMITED
PO BOX 1197
PORT TOWNSEND, WA 98368**

Name _____

Address _____

City/State/Zip _____

We accept Visa, Discover, and MasterCard. For credit card orders *only,* call 1-800-380-2230, 24 hours a day, 7 days a week.
Web site:www.loompanics.com